Practical Guide to the Operational Use of the HK G3/HK91 Rifle

By Erik Lawrence

Copyright© 2017 Erik Lawrence

Erik Lawrence
www.vig-sec.com   erik@vig-sec.com

Printed and bound in the United States of America

First printing 2017

ISBN: 978-1-961989-11-5
eBook ISBN: 978-1-961989-13-9

ATTENTION U.S. MILITARY UNITS, U.S. GOVERNMENT AGENCIES, AND PROFESSIONAL ORGANIZATIONS: Quantity discounts are available on bulk purchases of this book. Special books or book excerpts can also be created to fit specific needs. For information, please contact

Erik Lawrence
www.vig-sec.com   erik@vig-sec.com

SAFETY NOTICE
Before starting an inspection, ensure the weapon is cleared. Do not manipulate the trigger until the weapon has been cleared of all ammunition. Inspect the chamber to ensure that it is empty and no ammunition is present. Keep the weapon oriented in a safe direction when loading and handling.

AMMUNITION NOTICE- Firing the incorrect ammunition will damage the weapon and possibly injure the operator.

Training should be received from knowledgeable and experienced operators on this weapons system. Vigilant Security Services, LLC® provides this training and continually perfects its instruction with up-to-date information from actual use.

www.vig-sec.com

Table of Contents

Section 1

Introduction

The objective of this manual is to allow the reader to be able to use the variants of the Heckler and Koch (HK)-designed G3/HK 91 rifle competently. The manual will give the reader background/specifications of the weapon, instructions on its operation, disassembly and assembly; proper firing procedure; and malfunction/misfire procedures. Operator-level maintenance will also be detailed to allow the reader to understand and become competent in the use and maintenance of the G3/HK 91 variants.

Figure 1-1 HK G3A3

Figure 1-2 HK G3A4

Description

The characteristics of the HK G3/HK 91:

A. Country of Origin: Germany

B. Military Designation: G3

C. Operation: Full- and semi-automatic fire

D. Cartridge: 7.62x51mm (.308 Winchester)

E. Length: See below for variations

    a. Fixed stock: G3A3

- 40 inches (1,025mm)

    b. Telescoping stock: G3A4

- 40 inches (1,025mm with stock extended/33 inches, 840mm with stock collapsed)

F. Barrel: 17.7 inches (450mm)

G. Weight (unloaded): See below for variations

    a. 9 lbs. (4.1kg) (G3A4)

    b. 10 lbs. (4.7kg) (G3A3)

H. Type of Feed: 20-round detachable box

I. Operating System: Delayed blowback, closed bolt

J. Rate of Fire: 500-600 rpm

K. Maximum Effective Range: 600 meters

Background

The G3 (which stands for Gewehr 3, or Rifle 3) is a family of select-fire battle rifles manufactured by Heckler & Koch. It was adopted as the standard service rifle in 1959 by the Bundeswehr, as well as several other countries. The G3 was chambered for the 7.62×51 mm NATO cartridge and was developed in 1956 by the German armament manufacturer Heckler & Koch GmbH (HK) in collaboration with the Spanish state-owned design and development agency CETME (*Centro de Estudios Técnicos de Materiales Especiales*).

HK was founded by Edmond Heckler, Alex Seidel and Theodore Koch, all former Mauser Werke employees. HK commenced operations in 1948 in Oberndorf/Neckar as a manufacturer of sewing machine parts and gauges for the machine tool industry.

The origin of this Rifle can be traced back to the final years of World War II when Mauser engineers at the Light Weapon Development Group (Abteilung 37) at Oberndorf/Neckar designed the *MKb Gerät 06* (*Maschinenkarabiner Gerät 06 or "machine carbine device 06"*) prototype assault rifle chambered for the intermediate 7.92x33mm Kurz cartridge, first with the Gerät 06 model using a roller-locked short-recoil mechanism originally adapted from the MG 42 machine gun, but with a fixed barrel and conventional gas-actuated piston rod. It was realized that with careful attention to the mechanical ratios, the gas system could be omitted. The resultant weapon, the Gerät 06H (the "H" suffix is an abbreviation for *halbverriegelt* or "half-locked") was assigned the designation StG 45(M) (*Sturmgewehr 45(M)* or assault rifle) but was not produced in any significant numbers, and the war ended before the first production rifles were completed.

The German technicians involved in developing the StG 45(M) were taken to work in France at CEAM (*Centre d'Etudes et d'Armement de Mulhouse*). The StG 45(M) mechanism was modified by Ludwig Vorgrimler and Theodor Löffler at the Mulhouse facility between 1946 and 1949. Three versions were made, chambered in .30 Carbine and 7.92x33mm Kurz as well as the experimental 7.65x35mm French short cartridge developed by Cartoucherie de Valence in 1948. A 7.5x38mm cartridge using a partial aluminium bullet was abandoned in 1947. Löffler's design, designated the *Carabine Mitrailleuse Modèle 1950*, was retained for trials among 12 different prototypes designed by CEAM, MAC, and MAS.

In 1950, Vorgrimler moved to Spain where he created the LV-50 rifle chambered for the Kurz cartridge and later, the proprietary 7.92x40mm CETME M53 round. At this point, the rifle was renamed the *Modelo 2*. The Modelo 2 drew the attention of the West German Border Guards (*Bundesgrenzschutz*), who sought to re-equip the newly formed national defense forces. Not willing to accept a cartridge outside of the NATO specification, the Germans asked CETME to develop a 7.62x51mm version of the rifle. The resulting CETME Model A was chambered for the 7.62x51mm CETME cartridge, which was identical in chamber dimensions but had a reduced-power load compared to the 7.62x51mm NATO round. Further development of the rifle with input from HK produced the CETME Model B, which received several modifications, including the ability to fire from a closed bolt in both semi-automatic and automatic firing modes, a new perforated sheet metal handguard (the folding bipod had been the foregrip in previous models), improved ergonomics and a slightly longer barrel with a 22mm rifle grenade launcher guide. In 1958, this rifle was accepted into service with the Spanish Army as the *Modelo 58*, using the 7.62x51mm CETME round.

In 1956, the *Bundesgrenzschutz* canceled their planned procurement of the CETME rifles, adopting the Belgian-made FN FAL (G1) instead. However, the newly formed West German Army (*Bundeswehr*) now showed interest and soon purchased many CETME Rifles (7.62x51mm NATO chambering) for further testing. The CETME, known as the *Automatisches Gewehr G3* per German nomenclature, competed successfully against the Swiss SIG SG 510 (G2) and the American AR-10 (G4) to replace the previously favored G1 rifle. In January 1959, the Bundeswehr officially adopted the CETME proposal. The West German government wanted the G3 Rifle to be produced under license in Germany; purchase of the G1 had previously fallen through over FN's refusal to grant such a license. In the case of the G3, the Dutch firm Nederlandse Wapen en Munitiefabriek (NWM) held production and sales rights to the CETME design outside of Spain. To acquire production rights, the West German government offered NWM contracts to supply the German Air Force (*Luftwaffe*) with 20mm ammunition. Production of the G3 was then assigned to Rheinmetall and HK. The latter company already had ties to CETME and had worked to further optimize the CETME rifle for use with the full-power 7.62x51mm NATO cartridge (as opposed to the downgraded CETME variant). In 1969, Rheinmetall gave up production rights to the G3 in exchange for HK's promise not to bid on MG 3 production. Later in 1977, the West German government ceded ownership of G3 production and sales rights exclusively to HK.

Initial production G3 rifles differed substantially from more recent models; early rifles featured closed-type mechanical flip-up sights (with two apertures), a lightweight folding bipod, a stamped sheet steel handguard, a wooden buttstock (in fixed-stock models), or a telescopic metal stock. The weapon was modernized during its service life (among other minor modifications, it received new sights, a different flash suppressor, and a synthetic handguard and shoulder stock), resulting in the most recent production models, the G3A3 (with a fixed polymer stock) and the G3A4 (telescoping metal stock). The rifle proved successful in the export market, being adopted by the armed forces of over 40 countries. The G3 was and in some cases, continues to be produced under license in France (MAS), Greece (Hellenic Arms Industry), Iran (Defense Industries Organization), Luxembourg (Luxemburg Defense Technologie), Mexico, Myanmar, Norway

(Kongsberg Våpenfabrikk), Pakistan (Pakistan Ordnance Factories), Portugal (FBP), Saudi Arabia, Sweden (FFV), Thailand, Turkey (MKEK), and the United Kingdom (Royal Ordnance).

Receiver Marking

Since the late 1970s, Heckler & Koch has employed a simple letter code marked on the top of the receiver, the bottom left side of all magazines, and some components, to indicate the year of manufacture. Given that "A" signifies zero, "B" means "1" and so on up to "J," which stands for "9," it's easy to date any HK weapon or magazine. For example, a receiver marked "IF" tells us that the firearm was produced in 1985.

Proof Mark – Six Proof Houses in Germany. **ULM is utilized by HK.**

| ULM | Berlin | Kiel | Hannover | Munich | Koln |

HK Date Code:

A = 0	B = 1	C = 2	D = 3	E = 4
F = 5	G = 6	H = 7	I = 8	K = 9

J is reserved for proof house and on HK parts not required to be proof tested, such as magazine housings.

Safety Lever Operation

Standard S-E-F (stands for S – *Sicher* - SAFE, E – *Einselfeuer* – Single shot, F – *Feuerstoss* – Burst of Fire)

The weapon is SAFE when set on "0," "S" (SAFE); the selector lever's spindle prevents all upward movement of the sear, and its nose cannot drop out of engagement with the hammer's notch.

When put on "1," "E" (*Einzeln* = single), pulling the trigger will rotate the sear down and out of the hammer's notch. When the hammer rotates forward, the sear slips forward, and its end drops down off a fixed step. In recoil, the hammer is rotated back by the bolt carrier and catches the sear's nose, pushing it back in contact with the fixed step. After the bolt closes again, the auto sear releases the hammer, which is then held by the sear. Releasing the trigger allows the tail end of the sear to rise and move onto the fixed step. Pulling the trigger again will repeat the process.

When the selector lever is set to "F" (*Feuerstoss* = burst/full-auto), the spindle allows the sear's tail to rise so high that the sear's nose does not engage the hammer notch at all. The hammer is thus held by the auto sear only. As soon as the bolt carrier moves completely forward, the auto sear is released, and the hammer set free.

The safety lever on the trigger group has three positions.

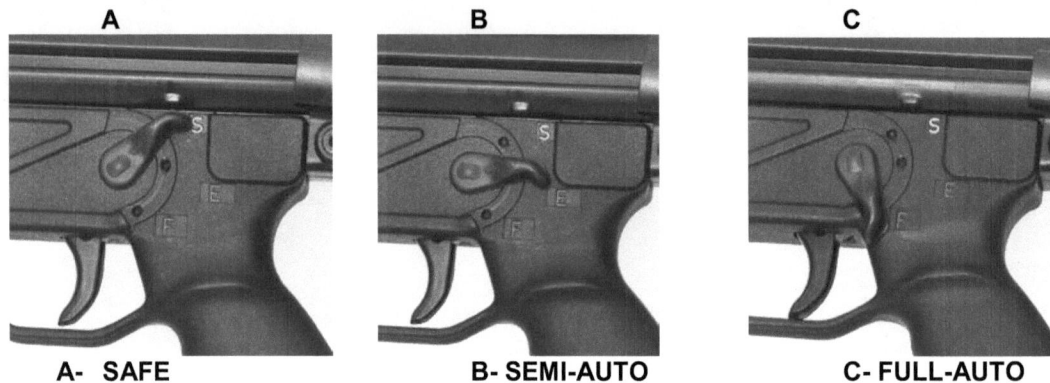

A	B	C
A- SAFE	B- SEMI-AUTO	C- FULL-AUTO

Figures 1-3 Photos of the selector lever in different positions

Sights

It should be noted that rotation of the rear sight on the G3 will bring into view apertures of different diameters only. Elevation remains constant. Elevation adjustments are made by inserting of a special tool with two spring-loaded wedges into the rear sight cylinder to engage two slots in the axis shaft that contain the spring-loaded catch bolts. When the catch bolts have been depressed, the sight cylinder can then be freely rotated around its threaded axis shaft in the desired direction. The tool also contains a Phillips-head screwdriver used to loosen the lock screw and turn the windage adjusting screw.

Once zero adjustments have been performed, there is little requirement for continued sight adjustment of a rifle. The well-protected front sight post is not adjustable. Best employed as a ghost ring, the largest rear aperture should be used always, except when engaging targets at longer ranges with semi-automatic fire. Self-luminous tritium front and rear sight inserts are available from HK as an option.

A- 100 meters   **B- 200 meters**   **C- 400 meters**

Figures 1-4 Photos of the sight drum in different positions

Nomenclature

Figure 1-5 Photo of the overall G3 RIFLE disassembled

1- Muzzle
4- Magazine Well
7- Trigger Group
10- Endcap
13- Bolt Head

2- Protected Front Sight
5- Magazine Release Lever
8- Locking Pins
11- Guide Rod/Recoil Spring
14- Locking Piece

3- Cocking Handle
6- Rear Sight
9- Buttstock
12- Firing Pin and Spring
15- Bolt Carrier

Figure 1-6 G3 trigger group

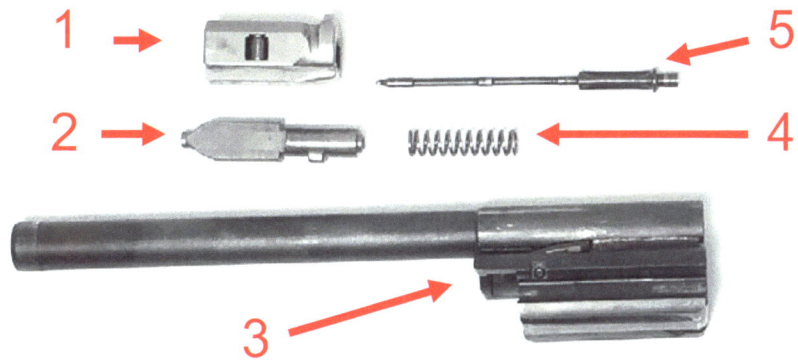

Figure 1-7 G3 bolt carrier assembly pieces

1- Bolt Head   2- Locking Piece   3- Bolt Carrier
4- Firing Pin Spring   5- Firing Pin

Variants

The G3 served as a basis for many other weapons, among them the PSG1 and MSG90 precision rifles, the HK11 and HK21 family of light machine guns, a semi-automatic version known as the HK41, a "sporterized" model called the SR9 (designed for the civilian market in countries where the HK91 would not qualify, primarily the US after the 1989 importation restrictions), and the MC51 carbine.

- **G3**: Original model based on the CETME Modelo B. It had a wooden stock and handguard.
- **G3A1**: G3 with a single-position, collapsible stock. This design was chosen after earlier experimentation with an MP-40 style ventrally folding metal stock; excessive recoil caused it to be dropped from consideration.
- **G3A2**: G3 with new rotating drum rear sight.
- **G3A3**: The most well-known version. Drum sights, a fixed plastic buttstock, and a plastic handguard that does not contact the barrel. The handguard came in a slim, ventilated version and a wide version. The latter allows for the attachment of a bipod.
- **G3A3A1**: This is a version of the G3A3 with an ambidextrous trigger group and brass deflector. This is an official German Army designation, not an HK factory one.
- **G3A4**: The G3A4 uses drum sights and a single position, collapsible stock. Entered service in 1974 for frontline infantry units.
- **G3A4A1**: This is a variant of the G3A4 with an ambidextrous trigger group and brass deflector. This is an official German Army designation, not an HK factory one.
- **G3KA4**: Smallest of the line, it is a *Karabiner*, or carbine version of the G3. It features drum sights, a retractable stock, and a 12.4 in./315mm barrel.
- **G3KA4A1**: Variant of the G3KA4 with an ambidextrous trigger group and brass deflector. This is an official German Army designation, not an HK factory one.

Models made under license

- **G3P3**: Model number for Pakistani-made version of G3A3.
- **G3P4**: Model number for Pakistani-made version of G3A4.
- **G3A5**: HK-assigned model number for the HK-made Danish version of the G3A3. It differs in that it has a silent bolt-closure device. In Danish service, it is known as the **Gv M/66**. The Gv M/66 was originally intended for use with optics as a designated marksman rifle, while the rest of the squad were issued M1 Garands.
- **G3A6**: HK-assigned model number for the Iranian-made version of the G3A3. It differs in having a dark-green handguard, stock, and trigger pack.

- **G3A7**: HK-assigned model number for the Turkish-made version of the G3A3.
- **G3A7A1**: HK-assigned model number for the Turkish-made version of the G3A4.
- **HSG1**: HK-assigned model number for the Luxembourg-made version of the G3A3.

Other Military Variants and Derivatives

Denmark

- **Gv M/75**: Variant leased from the German Bundeswehr/German government by the Danish government to replace the aging M1 Garands. Originally manufactured by either Rheinmetall or HK for the German Bundeswehr. The Gv M/75 rifles are basically G3s with the old-style straight cocking tube as opposed to the later FS (*Freischwinger*, "Cantilevered") variant. The Rheinmetall versions lack an external selector lever and can be converted from semi-automatic to full automatic (or vice versa) using a special tool.

Norway

- **AG-3**: Norwegian G3A5 variant produced by Kongsberg Våpenfabrikk, with the given name *Automatgevær 3*. A total of 253,497 units were produced for the Norwegian Armed Forces from 1967 to 1974. The Norwegian AG-3 differs from the original G3; the bolt carrier has a serrated thumb groove to aid in silent bolt closure, it features an all-metal cocking handle and a different bayonet mount. In 2007, it was announced that the AG-3 would be replaced by the Heckler & Koch HK416, in all military branches except for certain groups of the Home Guard.
- **AG-3F1**: An AG-3 with a retractable stock as on G3A4. Produced by Kongsberg Våpenfabrikk. A retractable stock was required by certain groups of soldiers within the Norwegian Armed Forces, primarily vehicle crews with limited space inside, particularly where a quick disembarkment from such a vehicle is required. All versions of the AG-3 have the ability to attach a 40mm HK79 grenade launcher.
- **AG-3F2**: An improvement of the AG-3F1, featuring B&T Picatinny rails on the receiver, as well as a RIS handguard. On the AG-3F2, Aimpoint red dot sights were mounted onto the receiver top rail for faster quick acquisition and easier aiming in low-light conditions.

Sweden

- **Ak 4**: Swedish-made version of the G3A3 with a buttstock that is approx. 2 cm longer. The bolt carrier has a serrated thumb groove to aid in silent bolt closure and is fitted with a heavy buffer for higher number of rounds

11

fired before failure. The rifles were manufactured from 1965 to 1970 by both Carl Gustafs Stads Gevärsfabrik and Husqvarna Vapenfabrik and from 1970 until the end of production in 1985 exclusively by Gevärsfabrik in Eskilstuna. All Ak 4s are adapted to mount the M203 grenade launcher. Sweden has supplied unmodified AK4s to Estonia, Latvia, and Lithuania.

- **Ak 4OR**: *Optiskt Riktmedel*, optical sight. This model is fitted with a Hensoldt 4x24 telescopic sight mounted via a HK claw mount. For a few years, it was not issued, but it is now again in use by the *Hemvärnet - Nationella skyddsstyrkorna* ("Swedish Home Guard").
- **Ak 4B**: In this updated version, the iron sights have been removed and replaced with an Aimpoint CS red-dot reflex sight mounted on a Picatinny rail. The rail is welded onto the rifle. Used by *Hemvärnet-Nationella skyddsstyrkorna* ("Swedish Home Guard").

In 2015, the Swedish Defence Materiel Administration, FMV, procured a new modular handguard and a new adjustable stock for the AK4; both items will be manufactured and supplied by the Swedish company Spuhr i Dalby AB.

- **Ak 4D**: DMR weapon for sharpshooting developed in 2016. New handguard and adjustable stock with a Hensoldt 4x24 telescopic sight.

Iran

- **DIO G3-A3 Bullpup**: Iranian bullpup variant of the G3.

Pakistan

- **G3P4**: Pakistan Ordnance Factory designation for license-produced G3A4 rifles.
- **G3S**: A version of G3P3 with a shorter barrel.
- **G3M-Tactical**: A light-weight version of G3 rifle with polymer body and shorter barrel.

United Kingdom

- **FR Ordnance MC51 Machine Carbine**: Produced by the UK firm FR Ordnance International Ltd. The MC51 weighs 6.8 lbs./3.1 kg, has a folded overall length of 24.6 inches/625mm, a barrel length of only 9.1 inches/230mm, which produces a muzzle velocity of approx. 2,263.8 fps/690 mps. Another UK-based company called Imperial Defence Services Ltd. absorbed FR Ordnance and continues to market the MC51 standard variant.

Specialized G3 Types

- **G3TGS**: This is simply a G3 with a 40mm HK79 under-barrel grenade launcher. TGS stands for *Tragbares Granat System* ("portable grenade system").
- **G3A3ZF**: This is a rifle issued with a claw-and rail scope bracket and a 4 x24mm Hensoldt scope. The ZF stands for *Zielfernrohr* or "telescopic sight."
- **G3SG/1**: An accurized variant of the G3. The "SG" stands for *Scharfschützengewehr* or "sharpshooting rifle." The rifles were individually selected from the production line for their accuracy and then modified. A Zeiss 1.5-6x variable power telescopic sight was added using an HK claw mount attached to the receiver. The stock was extended slightly compared to the standard G3 fixed stock and comes with a heavy, dual-stage buffer and adjustable cheek rest. A special set trigger group was added for a crisp trigger pull of 1 lb. Automatic fire was retained.
- **MSG3**: A variant featuring the newer scope mount that is found on only a few of the Heckler & Koch rifles, as compared to the more conventional claw mounts, though the claw mounting points remain on the receiver. This newer scope mount does not allow the use of the open sights with the mount in place, as is the case with the more conventional claw mount.
- **PSG-1**: A free-floating barrel semi-auto only version of the G3 with numerous other upgrades and such to meet the necessities of police sniper units. This rifle is famous for its accuracy and comfort, but infamous for its price and inability to be deployed by military units because some upgrades made the rifle too fragile.
- **MSG-90**: A somewhat cheaper version of the PSG-1 modified for military applications.
- **HK32**: An experimental variant of the rifle chambered for the Soviet 7.62x39mm M43 cartridge. It was never adopted by any country.

Law enforcement and civilian models

- **G3A1***: The terminology used by custom gunsmiths (e.g., Choate) and importers (e.g., Interarms) for imported semi-automatic G3 weapons with an aftermarket side-folding stock. This is not part of official HK nomenclature.
- **HK41**: The HK41 is a semi-automatic version of the G3 that was marketed to law enforcement. Limited sales at home and US import restrictions and firearms regulations led this weapon to be dropped from HK's product line quickly, and it was replaced by the HK91.
- **Fleming Arms HK51**: Contrary to popular belief, the HK51 is not made by H&K, being a creation of the American Class II manufacturing after-market. The HK51 has no real standards but is usually a cut-down and modified G3A3 or its semi-automatic clones the HK41 and HK91 and modified to take MP5 furniture and accessories. It is usually fitted with a

13

collapsible stock and an 8.3 in./211mm long barrel; it is relatively small at 23.2 inches/590mm with the stock retracted and 30.7 in./780mm with the stock extended. The first commercial version was by Bill Fleming of Fleming Arms and existed before Heckler & Koch made the HK53.

- **HK91**: The HK91 is a semi-automatic version of the G3 like the HK41, also marketed to civilians. However, to comply with US firearm regulations, several modifications to the HK91 were made that do not appear on the first pattern HK41. Internal parts that could allow fully automatic fire were removed. A shelf was welded onto the receiver where the push-pin of the trigger pack would normally go to prevent installation of a fully automatic trigger pack. This did not allow the use of the paddle-style magazine release, and so the magazine release button on the right side of the magazine well must be used instead. It is otherwise identical to the G3A3/A4. Importation into the United States began in 1974 and ceased in 1989, with some 48,000 rifles being imported.
- **HK911**: The HK911 was an HK91A2 with the flash hider removed and the receiver re-stamped with an extra 1 to comply with the US importation ban of 1989. The new designation theoretically made it legally immune to the Import Ban, as no "HK911" rifles were mentioned on the list of banned guns. However, the later banning of several "paramilitary" features on the HK911 made it illegal.
- **SR9**: These variants of the HK91ZF were created to comply with the Semi-Auto Import Ban of 1989, which included all variants of the HK91. They differed from the HK91 in that they had their flash hiders removed and featured a smooth fore end that lacked the bipod attachment point. The SR9 series was banned from importation to the United States because the variants could accept standard-capacity magazines. The SR9 was an HK91A2ZF with the pistol grip and buttstock replaced with a one-piece thumbhole stock.
  - **SR9 (T)**: The (T) or "Target" model was an HK91A2ZF with the trigger replaced with the PSG-1 model, the pistol grip replaced with an ergonomic PSG-1 grip, and the buttstock replaced with an MSG90 model.
  - **SR9 (TC)**: The (TC) or "Target Competition" model was an HK91A2ZF with the trigger group, pistol grip, and buttstock derived from the PSG-1.

Other Manufacturers

- **PTR91 Series**: Additionally, JLD (now PTR Industries) started manufacturing semi-automatic copies of the HK G3 called the PTR 91 in the United States. They used tooling from the FMP arms factory in Portugal to build the rifles.
- **Century International Arms**: Century Arms builds a clone of the G3 under the model designation of C308.

- **SAR-3**: Semi-automatic copy of HK-91 made by EBO in Greece and imported into the United States by Springfield Armory.
- **SAR-8**: Post-ban version of SAR-3, modified to comply with import restrictions.
- **Pakistan Ordnance Factories** produced under license from HK.

HK33/43/53

Figure 1-8 HK 33

Caliber: 5.56x45 mm NATO

Type: Delayed blowback, closed-bolt

Overall length: 36 inches (920mm)

Weight unloaded: 8.4 lb. (3.8 kg)

Barrel length: 17 inches (431mm)

Magazine capacity: 5-, 20-, 25-, 30- or 40-round double column, detachable box magazine

Rate of Fire: Semi-Automatic

Maximum Effective Range: 500 meters

In the mid to late 1960s, Heckler & Koch developed the HK33, which was a scaled-down version of the Heckler Koch G3, but chambered for 5.56x45mm NATO. The HK33 entered production in 1968. In 1974, a semi-automatic version of the HK33 was introduced by H&K and was designated the HK43. Per HK's numbering nomenclature, the "4" indicates that the weapon is a paramilitary rifle, and the "3" indicates that the caliber is .223.

- HK33A2- Variant with a rigid synthetic stock.

- HK33SG/1- An accurized model; equipped with a telescopic sight and improved trigger analogous to the one used in the G3SG/1.

- HK33A3- Standard rifle but with telescoping metal stock.

- HK33KA3- Carbine version with barrel reduced in length to the base of the front sight post; also, equipped with a folding metal stock. Due to the short barrel, the

- HK33KA3 cannot be used to launch rifle grenades or mount a bayonet.

- HK53- Compact version of the HK33K. Has a short, 8.5 inch/211mm barrel, a forearm derived from the MP5 submachine gun, and a telescopic shoulder stock or receiver endplate cover (later models also received a four-prong flash hider).

- HK13- Light machine gun. It is fed from either box or drum magazines (the latter has a 100-round capacity), has a quick-change heavy barrel for sustained fire, is shrouded with a sheet metal heat guard (replacing the synthetic forearm), and has a 2-point bipod adapter.

- Type 11- A derivative of the HK33 manufactured in Thailand by the Ministry of National Defence for use by the Thai armed forces. A bullpup variant also exists, with M16 sights and foregrip for close combat in jungle environments

CETME Model 58

Figure 1-9 CETME Model 58

Caliber: 7.62x51 mm NATO

Type: Delayed blowback, closed bolt

Overall length: 40 inches (1010mm)

Weight unloaded: 9.9 pounds (4.5kg)

Barrel length: 18 inches (450mm)

Magazine capacity: 20-round double column, detachable box magazine

Rate of Fire: Select Fire and Semi-Automatic models

Maximum Effective Range: 600 meters

The **CETME Model 58** is a stamped-steel, select-fire battle rifle produced by the Spanish armaments manufacturer Centro de Estudios Tecnicos de Materiales Especiales (CETME). The Model 58 used a 20-round box magazine and was chambered for the 7.62x51mm NATO round (although originally designed for the reduced power Spanish 7.62x51mm cartridge). The CETME 58 would become the foundation of the widely deployed German Heckler & Koch G3 battle rifle. Semi-automatic variants were also produced for the civilian market.

HK PSG1

Figure 1-10 HK PSG1

Caliber: 7.62x51 mm NATO

Type: Delayed blowback, closed bolt

Overall length: 48.5 inches (1230mm)

Weight unloaded: 16 pounds (7.2kg)

Barrel length: 25.5 inches (650mm)

Magazine capacity: 5-, 10- and 20-round double column, detachable box magazine

Rate of Fire: Semi-Automatic

Maximum Effective Range: 1,000 meters

The PSG1 (*Präzisionsschützengewehr*, German for "precision shooting rifle") is a semi-automatic sniper rifle designed by the German company Heckler & Koch of Oberndorf am Neckar.

The **PSG1A1** variant was introduced by Heckler & Koch in 2006 and features two major improvements. First, the cocking handle was relocated a couple of degrees counter-clockwise, since when locked rearward, it could physically interfere with the long scopes often used on the rifles. The second modification involved the replacement of the outdated Hensoldt scope. Non-police users often found the scope's 600 m range limitation and simple crosshairs inadequate for their needs. In addition, the rechargeable batteries are difficult to recharge and to find as replacements. A final fault is that Hensoldt does not service the scope in the United States. For these reasons, the PSG1A1 has been outfitted with a Schmidt & Bender 3-12x50 Police Marksman II scope, mounted on 1.3 in./34mm rings. One last modification involved converting the SG 550 Sniper stock to work with the PSG1. The HK rifle now has a completely side-folding adjustable target stock removing a solid 10 in./250mm in overall length. To remedy brass ejection, a brass catcher must be installed.

19

Section 2

Maintenance

Clearing the G3 Rifle

Figure 2-1 G3 rifle Selector in the SAFE position

A. Ensure the rifle is on SAFE and pointed in a safe direction.

Figure 2-2a   **Figure 2-2b**

B. Remove the magazine by pressing the magazine release lever forward (military version) or push the magazine release button (civilian) (Figure 2-2a) and pull the magazine from the magazine well (Figure 2-2b). Place the magazine in a pocket, magazine pouch or set it down.

 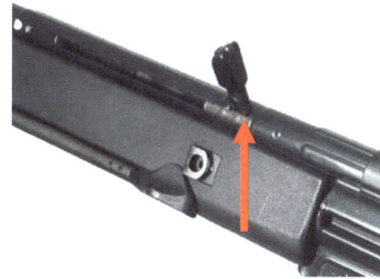

Figure 2-3a	**Figure 2-3b**

C. Pull the cocking handle to the rear (Figure 2-3a) and up to lock the bolt to the rear (Figure 2-3b). Observe the round extracting and ejecting from the ejection port; do not attempt to retain the round.

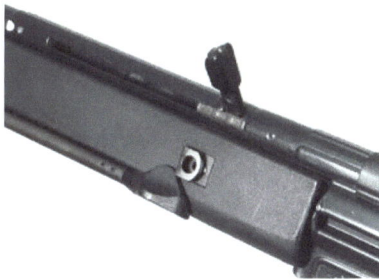 

Figure 2-4a	**Figure 2-4b**

D. With the cocking handle locked in the open positon (Figure 2-4a), now visually check the chamber for a round (Figure 2-4b).

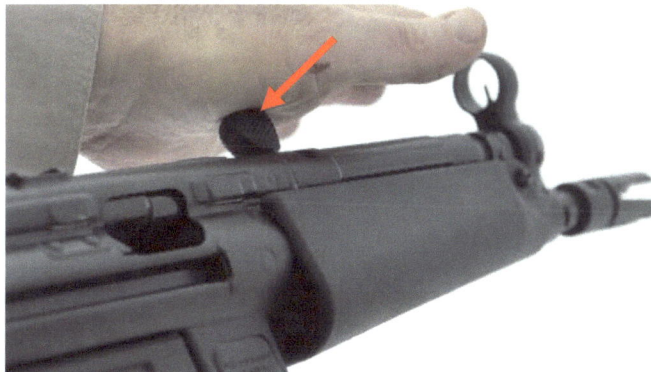

Figure 2-5

E. Once you have ensured the rifle has no magazine in it and the chamber is free of a round, you now can close the bolt by hitting the charging handle down to remove it from the locking notch (Figure 2-5).

Disassembling the G3 Rifle

NOTE- Place the rifle's parts on a flat, clean surface with the muzzle oriented in a safe direction.

When the operator begins to disassemble the rifle, it should be done in the following order:

Figure 2-6a **Figure 2-6b**

A. Remove the locking pin in the rear of the receiver (Figures 2-6a & 2-6b); place them in the stock holes or the hole it came from on the buttstock so they are not misplaced.

Figure 2-7a

Figure 2-7b

B. Remove the buttstock/butt cap (Figures 2-7a & 2-7b).

Figure 2-8

C. Rotate the trigger assembly down and off the receiver (Figure 2-8).

Figure 2-9

D. Pull/push the charging handle to the rear to begin to remove the bolt assembly (Figure 2-9).

Figure 2-10a

Figure 2-10b

E. Remove the bolt assembly (Figures 2-10a & 2-10b), using the charging handle as necessary.

Figure 2-11

F. Slide the bolt head forward (Figure 2-11) until the top tabs meet and the rollers will retract into the bolt head.

Figure 2-12a

Figure 2-12b

G. Rotate the bolt head just until the top tab clears (Figure 2-12a) and allow the bolt head to be slid forward off the locking piece (Figure 2-12b). If you rotate the bolt head too far to the right, the spring tension of the firing pin spring will eject the head off the carrier; if so, you are ahead.

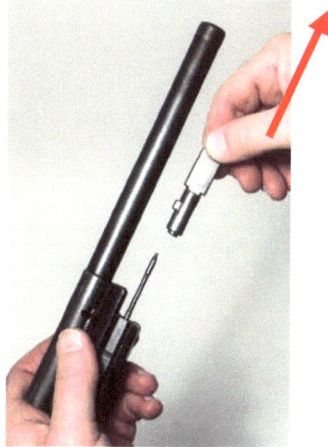

Figure 2-13a

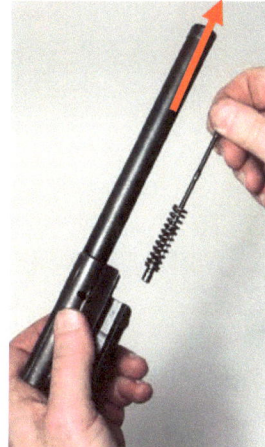

Figure 2-13b

H. Rotate the locking piece cam lobe so that it is down and can be removed from the bolt carrier (Figure 2-13a) and remove the firing pin and spring from the bolt carrier (Figure 2-13b).

LOCKING PIECE

The locking piece angles are critical to the proper function and safety of the gun; don't grind or use a stone on them.

Figure 2-14a

Figure 2-14b

I. Remove the forearm locking pin (Figure 2-14a) and the handguard (Figure 2-14b) as needed; retain the pin back into the forearm.

Reassembling the G3 Rifle

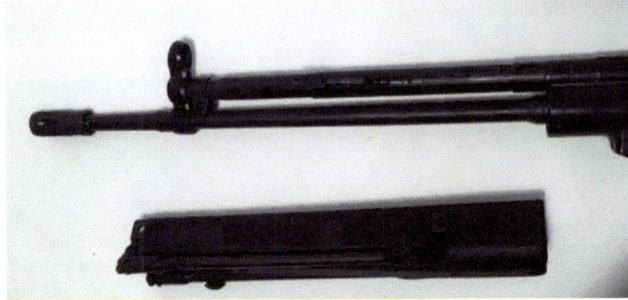

Figure 2-15a

Figure 2-15b

A. Place the forearm back on the rifle if removed for disassembly (Figures 2-15a and 2-15b).

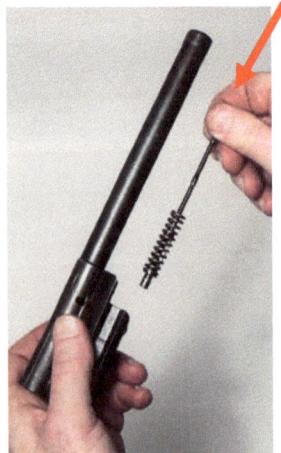

Figure 2-16

B. Holding the bolt carrier up, insert the firing pin onto its spring and into the bolt carrier (firing pin tip up) (Figure 2-16).

Figure 2-17

C. Insert into the locking piece (Figure 2-17), oriented with the locking lobe down.

Figure 2-18

D. Place the locking piece with the firing pin and spring into the bolt carrier with the cam lobe down, press in, and slightly rotate it LEFT- just less than 180 degrees (Figure 2-18).

Figure 2-19a

Figure 2-19b

Figure 2-19c

Figure 2-19d

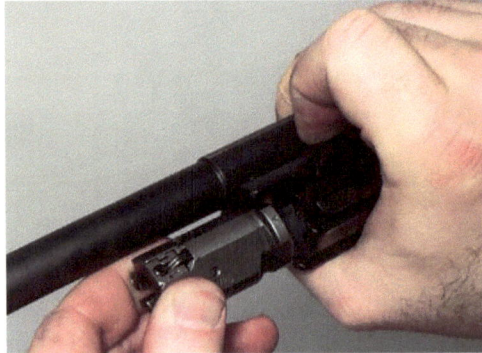

Figure 2-19e

E. Place the bolt head onto the locking piece (Figure 2-19a), aligning it so the ramp of the bolt head is against the spring-loaded locking lever (Figure 2-19b); press down until the ramp pushes up the spring-loaded locking lever (Figure 2-19c); and then rotate the bolt head to the right into the locked position (Figure 2-19d). You may need to modify this by pressing in on the spring-loaded lever to get the bolt head to more easily slide on the ramp and into position (Figure 2-19e).

Figure 2-20a   **Figure 2-20b**   **Figure 2-20c**

F. To unlock the rollers in the bolt head, place the inverted (backwards) bolt carrier group into the back of the receiver (Figure 2-20a) and lightly slam down to have the receiver press the rollers into the unlocked position (Figure 2-20b). Pull the bolt carrier group out of the receiver, and it is ready to be fully inserted for assembly (Figure 2-20c).

Figure 2-21

G. Orient the muzzle down and slide the bolt carrier assembly into the receiver, bolt head first (Figure 2-21).

Figure 2-22a   **Figure 2-22b**

29

H. Place the front of the trigger assembly into the bottom notch on the receiver (Figure 2-22a) and rotate upwards (Figure 2-22b); ensure the hammer is cocked and the trigger assembly is flush with the bottom of the receiver so the end cap will fit on.

Figure 2-23

I. Remove the locking pins from the stock and place the stock/butt cap onto the rear of the receiver (Figure 2-23); then align and insert the pins to retain the trigger assembly. If the stock rails are not aligning then slightly collapse the stock and align the buttcap to seat it.

Performing a Function Check on the G3 Rifle

Ensure there is no magazine in the weapon; clear the rifle prior to performing a function check.

A. Pull the cocking handle to the rear and release. Ensure the selector lever is on SAFE and pull the trigger. The hammer should not fall.

B. Place the selector lever on SEMI. Pull the trigger and hold it to the rear. The hammer should fall.

C. Pull the cocking handle to the rear and release. Release the trigger, hear the reset, and pull the trigger again. The hammer should fall.

D. Pull the cocking handle to the rear and release. Place the selector lever on AUTO. Pull the trigger and hold it to the rear. The hammer should fall.

E. Pull the cocking handle to the rear several times and release. Release the trigger and pull it again. The hammer should not fall.

F. Pull the cocking handle to the rear, release, and pull the trigger. The hammer should fall.

G. Pull the cocking handle to the rear and release. Place the selector lever on SAFE.

Maintenance of the Magazine

A. Disassembly
   a. Push the locking plate into the magazine housing.
   b. Press tabs in and remove the floor plate.
   c. Remove the follower spring, follower, and the locking plate.

When the magazine is disassembled, remove any dust, dirt, or foreign material from the magazine body and wipe off all the parts.

B. Assembly
   a. Insert the follower, magazine spring, and the locking plate into the magazine body and push the locking plate into the magazine.
   b. Place the floor plate onto the magazine.

Section 3

Operation and Function

Cycle of Function
1. Feeding
2. Chambering
3. Locking
4. Firing
5. Unlocking
6. Extracting
7. Ejecting
8. Cocking

Loading the G3 Magazine

NOTE- Ensure you have appropriate ammunition for the model to be used. Inspect it for uniformity, cleanliness, and serviceability. Check all cartridges for undented primers and only use issued ammunition.

1. Load cartridges into the magazine.

Figure 3-1a   **Figure 3-1b**
Magazine hand-loading procedure

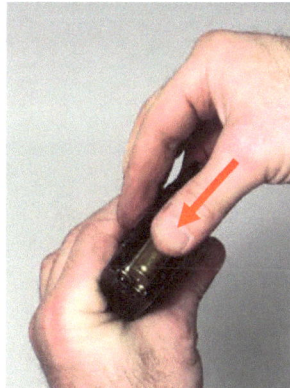

A. Use your non-dominant hand to hold the magazine with the front of the magazine toward your fingertips and your thumb as a guide on the rear of the magazine. With your dominant hand, one at a time, place the cartridge over the top of the magazine follower between the feed lips and press the cartridge straight down until it snaps under the feed lips. Once the cartridge is under the lip of the magazine body, slide it fully to the rear so the next round will be allowed to be pushed down (Figures 3-1a and 3-1b).

B. Load 20 and then load the chamber so you have 19 in the magazine and one in the chamber and just 20 rounds in magazines you load from your pouches. The easiest approach is to lay out the number of rounds for each magazine so you don't have to count the rounds as you load the magazine.

Loading the Magazine into a G3 Rifle

Figure 3-2

A. With the RIFLE pointed in a safe direction, on SAFE, and the bolt locked to the rear (Figure 3-2),

Figure 3-3a

Figure 3-3b

B. insert the loaded magazine into the magazine well (Figure 3-3a). Pull down on the magazine with the loading hand to ensure it is locked in by the magazine catch (Figure 3-3b).

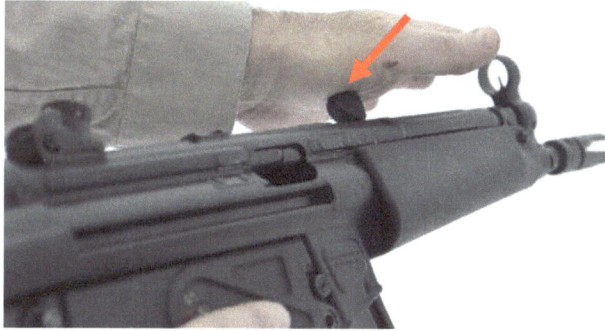
Figure 3-4

C. Slap down onto the top of the cocking handle (Figure 3-4) while sliding into the down position to release it from the locking notch on the receiver, allowing the full spring tension to close the bolt. Listen for everything seating and look to see that the bolt is fully forward and in battery.

D. To perform a press check, you can remove the magazine and see if the alternate bullet is at the top of the magazine. A loaded mag has a top right-side round, and once you chamber a round, the mag will now have a top left-side round. Ensure you lock the magazine back into the magazine well with a tug to ensure it is locked by the magazine catch.

Firing the G3 Rifle

A. Orient downrange or towards the threat.

B. Rotate the safety lever down to the desired mode of fire with a thumb.

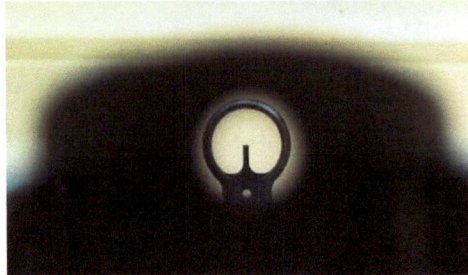

Figure 3-5 G3 Sight alignment

C. As you orient your sights onto the target, press the trigger straight back so as not to interrupt the sight alignment with the sight picture (Figure 3-5). If firing single shots, release the trigger only forward enough to reset the trigger, and then press it straight to the rear if another shot is needed. If firing full automatic, practice how long you hold the trigger for the desired burst and the recoil management required to keep the group on the desired target.

D. When you have completed firing the rifle, place the safety lever into the SAFE (up) position.

Firing positions for the FAL Rifle

Figure 3-6
Photo of standing position

Figure 3-7
Photo of kneeling position

Figure 3-8a Photo of prone position

Figure 3-8a Photo of prone position with bipod use

Figure 3-9 Supported barricade position

Section 4

Performance Problems

Malfunction and Immediate Action Procedures

Malfunctions are usually preventable through good practices, but they may still occur out of the blue from time to time. Of course, you hope it is on the practice range, but you should treat each one as though you are in a life-or-death situation. Practicing proper and effective corrective actions will allow you to be more confident in your weapon handling. In stressful situations, you can become much more stressed due to an unforeseen malfunction that is easy to correct. I have observed many shooters that perceive themselves to be experienced, who, when they encounter a stovepipe, nearly disassemble the weapon rather than sweep it out and continue.

Malfunction drills must fix the problem 100% of the time (excluding a weapon stoppage — broken weapon) the first time performed. You must look at the rifle and identify the problem (obviously, the rifle is not functioning as you need, so you must transition to another weapon or rectify the situation). It is a non-functioning weapon at this point — fix it.

You should always practice taking a covered position to correct malfunctions with considerations on how you operate.

The following pages in this chapter describe and detail corrective actions for the various malfunctions that may be encountered.

MALFUNCTION	CAUSE	CORRECTION
1. Failure to Feed	Magazine – Dirty	Clean
	- Dented	Replace
	- Lips Bent	Replace
	- Spring Broken	Replace spring
	- Loaded Wrong	Reload
	- Not Seated	Reseat
	Recoil Spring Broken/Bent	Replace
	Weapon Dirty	Clean
2. Failure to Chamber	Chamber Fouled	Clean
	Barrel Extension Fouled	Clean
	Deformed Cartridge	Pull back cocking handle and rechamber
	Weak or Broken Recoil Spring	Replace
	Receiver Bent	Replace
3. Failure to Lock	Missing Rollers	Inspect for damage Replace rollers
4. Failure to Fire	Firing Pin or Spring Broken	Replace
	Bolt not fully Locked	Recock and attempt to fire
5. Failure to Extract	Chamber Fouled	Clean
	Extractor Broken	Clean
6. Failure to Eject	Extractor/Ext. Spring Broken	Replace
	Extractor Spring Weak	Replace
	Ejector Broken	Replace
7. Failure to Cock	Hammer Broken	Replace
8. Recoil Hard	Bolt Carrier Striking Back Plate	Replace Buffer

FAILURE-TO-GO-INTO BATTERY:

NOTE: The <u>failure-to-go-into-battery malfunction</u>, when your bolt assembly does not fully return forward when cycling a round, is always rectified in the same manner. This malfunction is usually induced when loading and not allowing the full recoil spring tension to shut the slide.

To fix a failure-to-go-into-battery malfunction, you must ensure your finger is off the trigger and outside the triggerguard, and then rotate the rifle to the right (ejection port to ground). Then pull the cocking handle to the rear with the non-firing hand. Let the round fall to the ground, and once the cocking handle is fully to the rear, release it to close by its own spring tension. Listen and look for it fully seating the next round from the magazine.

FAILURE TO FIRE: This malfunction occurs when the operator has loaded a dud cartridge or failed to load the chamber. The universal fix all for this is the "<u>Slap</u>, <u>Rack</u>, <u>Bang</u>" technique.

SYMPTOM - You perform a full presentation to shoot and hear and feel the hammer strike, and the weapon does not fire.

CORRECTION:
1. **SLAP** – the bottom of the magazine with a hard palm (fingers extended) to ensure it is fully seated and locked in.

2. **RACK** – the cocking handle fully to the rear and release it to shut by its own recoil spring tension. You can pivot the rifle toward your non-firing hand to assist in racking the cocking handle to the rear; maintain muzzle to threat orientation.

3. **BANG** – or represent and prepare to fire the shot as you intended before the malfunction if your situation dictates that action.

FAILURE TO EJECT: This malfunction (commonly called a "stovepipe") is usually created by the bolt being retarded in its rearward movement to rechamber the next round or a weak extractor spring. This malfunction is easily corrected by ejecting the expended case from the port by turning the RIFLE ejection port to the ground and cycling the action.

SYMPTOM - You are in the act of shooting a multiple-round engagement, and you notice you felt the bolt assembly did not fully close, and/or have a soft, mushy trigger.

CORRECTION:
With the non-firing hand, extend your fingers, and with fingers joined, reach for the cocking handle. (DO NOT SWEEP YOUR HAND IN FRONT OF THE MUZZLE.) Roll your fingers around the cocking handle and with a firm, vigorous sweeping motion to the rear, pull the cocking handle to the rear while orienting

the ejection port to the ground. Roll the rifle left and look into the ejection port, and there should be no loose rounds. If there is a round in the magazine (if not, reload or transition to your pistol), release the cocking handle to close on its own spring tension and reorient to the threat.

Once the casing is no longer pinched by the bolt, the release of the cocking handle will continue to seat the next round, and you are now ready to continue the engagement. Many inexperienced shooters do too much to correct this simple malfunction.

FAILURE TO EXTRACT: This malfunction (commonly called a "double feed") is created when the spent casing is not extracted from the chamber (may be due to a damaged extractor or weak extractor spring), and the next round to be loaded is rammed from the magazine into the rear of the stuck casing. This malfunction is a serious one since more complicated dexterity is needed to correct it and, of course, to do it quickly. Below is the breakdown of the corrective action to restore your rifle back to operation.

SYMPTOM - You are shooting a multiple-shot engagement and notice your slide did not go forward; you have a soft, mushy trigger, and it will not fire.

CORRECTION:
STEP ONE – With the non-firing hand, extend your fingers, and with fingers joined, reach for the cocking handle. Roll your fingers around the cocking handle, and with a firm, vigorous sweeping motion to the rear, pull the cocking handle to the rear while orienting the ejection port to the ground. Roll the rifle to the left and look into the ejection port and there should be no loose rounds. If there is a round in the magazine and no loose round/cases, just release the cocking handle to close on its own spring tension and reorient to the threat. If a round is present, move to the next step.

STEP TWO – Lock the bolt to the rear and remove the magazine from the rifle.

STEP THREE – Rack the bolt to the rear at least two times to ensure the casing is extracted and ejected from the rifle. As you are doing this step, observe the casing being ejected and allow the action to use its spring tension to shut each time it is pulled to the rear.

STEP FOUR – Properly insert and seat a loaded magazine.

STEP FIVE – Hit the cocking handle down to release it to close by its own spring tension. Your rifle is now ready to continue the engagement.

STEP SIX – Continue the engagement as the situation dictates.

NOTE: Correcting this malfunction needs to be practiced often since it is the most complicated to do under stress or when you lose dexterity because blood is leaving the extremities.

www.ingramcontent.com/pod-product-compliance
Lightning Source LLC
Chambersburg PA
CBHW061057090426
42742CB00002B/75